Healthy to the Core!

All Natural
Low Sugar/No Sugar
Apple Recipes
For Kids

Lee Jackson

All inquiries should be addressed to:

Images Unlimited Publishing
P.O. Box 305
Maryville, MO 64468
660–582–4605

info@imagesunlimitedpublishing.com
http://www.imagesunlimitedpublishing.com

ATTN: Quantity discounts are available to your Educational Institution, Organization, Corporation, or Industry for reselling, educational purposes, subscription incentives, gifts or fund raising campaigns.

For more information, please contact the publisher at
Images Unlimited Publishing, 124 N. Grand Ave., Maryville, MO 64468
800–366–1695 Lee@imagesunlimitedpub.com

First Edition
10 9 8 7 6 5 4 3 2

Library of Congress Cataloging-in-Publication Data

Jackson, Lee (Leona)
   Healthy to the core! : all natural low sugar/no sugar apple recipes for kids / Lee Jackson. — First edition.
      pages cm
   Includes index.
   ISBN 978-0-930643-29-4 (alk. paper)
   1. Cooking (Apples) 2. Sugar-free diet—Recipes. I. Title.
   TX813.A6J3325 2013
   641.6'411—dc23
                                        2013026789

Printed in the United States of America
Interior drawings by Terri Wilson
Cover & Interior page design by MK Bassett-Harvey, LinesAreDrawn.com

Table of Contents

Introduction

Hi!

I'm very pleased to offer you this collection: *Healthy to the Core! All Natural Low Sugar/No Sugar Apple Recipes For Kids.* Your parents and grandparents will be interested in seeing where you are getting all the delicious apple recipes. I give you permission to share with them.

This is my third apple cookbook. Can you tell I love apples?

I've been an apple–lover all my life. There is always something new and interesting about apples. Sometimes it's a new variety with its unique flavor. Other times it's a way of using apples with a whole new twist.

The apple tree works hard to produce its fruit. In the spring the tree wakes up from its winter nap. Soon its pink buds and blossoms show off their royal beauty. Then, in the hot days of summer, the apples grow bigger and bigger. (The tree branches make an ideal spot for sitting and thinking). The fall hustle and bustle of apple season is filled with orchard trips and lots of apple tasting. In the winter, it's time to rest and get ready for another year. Each year is different yet the same.

I invite you to come along to the kitchen with me. We'll check out different apple tastes and cook up lots of apple

dishes. I'll help you make tasty apple recipes without lots of added sweeteners.

Keep in mind some apples are naturally sweeter than others. This is one of the fun and interesting challenges about working with apples. Some apples are sweet and some are sour.

Cooking with apples is not an exact science. Sometimes you have to use your own good thinking skills in deciding whether the product will be sweet enough or too sweet.

Then too, one's taste buds get overly dependent on sugar's sweet flavor and taste. They keep saying, *"I–like it and I–want–more!"* But the good part is, the less sugar you eat, the less your body "wants" it … simply amazing! In time, you may even find you don't need your food to be as sweet as you once did.

These recipes are not dependent on lots of sugar. By using less sugar you become more aware of the natural flavor of apples. Apples in themselves have wonderful flavors if time is taken to savor them.

So, come and take a tour through my apple orchard and on into the kitchen. May you have a good time experimenting with, and enjoying, apples.

My wish is that these recipes bring you joy and healthful good eating for you and your family.

Lu Jackson

In Appreciation

I could not possibly have produced this cookbook without the generous and ongoing support of many others. With thanks and appreciation to the many who supported and made this collection possible and to those who tested recipes, Amy Houts, Shirley Laughlin, Gayle Hull, Nancy Kendrew, Debbie Mack, Beth Sommers, Joan Osborne, Pat Taylor, Marion Harvey, I give my thanks. Your help and support were tremendously important.

When working with apples I never fail to appreciate the work of orchardists and horticulturalists. Many of our tastiest apples come from apple growers who have spent their entire lives perfecting their produce and taking pride in their work. It's not by chance that apples are a feast for the eyes and mouth.

Healthy Food Practices

The goal of this cookbook is to help you enjoy apples in their healthy organic form, but also to provide general guidelines about making healthy food choices. Here are my 10 top tips on what I consider the most important healthy food practices:

Top 10 Healthy Tips for Kids and Families:

1. Primarily eat fresh, unprocessed plants such as vegetables, fruits, nuts, and seeds, preferably locally grown, organic, and in season.

2. Avoid virtually all processed, manufactured foods and beverages, including fruit drinks and soda pop.

3. Eat a wide variety of food.

4. Eliminate or vastly reduce grains, especially wheat, from your diet. Wheat contains gluten as a protein that can cause an inflammation response in the body.

5. Minimize or eliminate pasteurized cow's milk products.

6. Eat good quality protein such as eggs and grass–fed beef and free–range and organic chicken, turkey and other poultry.

7. Cut out refined sugars and white flour.

8. Eliminate unhealthy oils such as corn oil, soy oil, and partially–hydrogenated oils.

9. Drink plenty of clean water.

10. Avoid GMO foods.

 Listen to your body. If you are low on energy, why is this? Think back on the food you have eaten. Also recall whether you are getting enough sleep and rest. Are you drinking enough water?

 The human body knows how to be healthy. You need to give it the right building materials to do its job. Unfortunately, much of all chronic disease is caused by poor food choices, toxic food ingredients, and lack of physical exercise.

The Big Four

From this list of healthy food practices, I've chosen to concentrate on what I call THE BIG FOUR:

 Avoid refined sugar

 Avoid white flour

 Avoid GMO products

 Use healthy cooking oil

 When compiling these recipes, I was very aware of the sugar and flours that go into baked products. Most apple recipes contain a great amount of both. But then I considered, *"Why can't these recipes be made with natural sweeteners and healthier kinds of flours?"* That is why I am providing a short summary of the suggested and preferred kinds of products to use when making apple recipes healthier.

Avoid Refined Sugar

It's too easy to get hooked on sugar. It's found in much of the food we eat. It goes by names such as white sugar, brown sugar, high fructose corn syrup, and powdered sugar. Sometimes it's referred to as table sugar. It is the most common sugar in use in our country. Unfortunately, all the healthy nutrients such as vitamins, minerals and enzymes have been removed in the refining process.

There are many problems associated with sugar. Your dentist tells you it's not good for your teeth. You've heard how sugar is a major contributor to weight gain. It's been linked to many serious health conditions such as diabetes, cancer, and even depression, mood swings, and brain "fog". Let's face it, too much sugar is bad for you.

This does not mean you should avoid all sweeteners. Wouldn't that make the world a dreary place? You can still get a sweet taste in food by using sweeteners that are less refined than table sugar while containing helpful vitamins or minerals. Isn't it better to get some nutritional benefits out of the sweeteners you use? I think so.

That is why I have used only natural sweeteners here in recipes I felt needed a bit of sweetness. I have used the following three natural sweeteners:

Organic evaporated cane sugar

honey

maple syrup

Organic evaporated cane sugar is basically dried sugar cane juice. Sucanat® is a brand name for a variety of whole

sugar cane. Sucanat stands for SUgar CAne NATural. Rapadura™ is another product made using the same process. These types of unrefined sugars can be purchased at your local health food store or organic market.

Organic evaporated cane sugar is made by crushing freshly cut sugar cane, squeezing out the juice and heating it in a large vat. Then it is allowed to cool, forming granular crystals. These are dark in color, and have a very distinctive and quite strong flavor. The molasses, or the good part of cane sugar, remains. It retains its' wonderful source of iron, as well as potassium, magnesium, and calcium. This unrefined sugar has nothing added and nothing taken out.

Sucanat® makes a good substitute for recipes that call for white or brown sugar. You can use the same amount of Sucanat® as the sugar called for in the recipe. It is especially good for baking.

Honey is a sweet food made by bees using nectar from flowers. It's mostly monosaccharides fructose and glucose and contains traces of potassium, calcium, and phosphorus. The kind and amount of nutrients depends on the flowers available to the bees that produced the honey.

When you're substituting honey for sugar in recipes, you need less honey than sugar because honey weighs more than sugar and is sweeter. It also has a different flavor than sugar.

Honey adds extra moisture to a recipe. Therefore, the other wet ingredients (milk, water, oil, eggs) need to be cut back in the recipe or else the product will be soggy.

All the recipes in this cookbook have been adjusted for this, but if you are using honey in other recipes, it is a good point to remember.

Young children under the age of 12 months should never be given honey in any form. It should not be added to their food, water, or formula, or even in baked or processed foods. It can make them sick because their bodies may not be able to fight off any possible reaction to or problem with honey.

When shopping for honey, try to find a local beekeeper who will be able to supply you with raw honey made by bees from your own area. Grocery stores often carry honey from local beekeepers. I encourage you to look up more information on honey and its benefits. It's a very remarkable product.

Maple syrup is the sap of the maple tree and comes directly from inside the tree. It is collected by drilling a hole in the tree and catching the sap in pails or though a tubing system. It is then heated at a high temperature to evaporate much of the water. This concentrated syrup is what we find bottled in the stores.

Maple syrup is a good substitute for table sugar. It is only 60% as sweet as sugar and is a source of manganese, zinc, and other nutrients. Maple syrup lends a darker texture and stronger flavor to baked goods.

This "real" maple syrup is usually quite expensive, as its production is limited to specific areas of the country. The amount gathered each spring is unpredictable because of weather conditions and the work in preparing it is extensive.

There are other natural sweeteners available but the above three are my favorites. I have used these three because I feel they are a healthier choice as they are less processed than white sugar. Other natural sweeteners not

included here are: palm sugar, date sugar, coconut sugar, maple sugar, brown rice syrup, molasses, stevia, agave nectar, and Xylitol.*

The amount of added natural sweeteners has been kept to a minimum in the following recipes. You will not find artificial sweeteners in this cookbook.

Avoid White Flour

White flour has been highly processed and refined, taking with it the nutrients originally found in the grain. Manufacturers often add synthetic vitamins and minerals, but it is still inferior to the whole grain. The refining is done to preserve its shelf life. If the flour doesn't have an expiration date on it, you know it can last indefinitely. Most "real" food tends to spoil after a period of time.

For most of these recipes the 'flour of choice' is whole wheat pastry flour. It has a smoother texture than whole wheat flour and can generally be used in the same ratio to white flour.

This type of flour has not been highly processed or refined. Some of the recipes for the baked goods may indicate rice flour or oat bran flour, but the majority work well with whole wheat pastry flour.

---

*For the cane sugar in these recipes I have used Sucanat® Cane Sugar, which is a certified organic, pure evaporated cane juice powder. It retains all the properties of natural sugar cane, including its molasses content, which gives it a strong and distinctive flavor. It converts as a 1 for 1 replacement of white or brown sugar.

Avoid GMO products

Genetically modified food (GMO's or GM foods or biotech foods) have specific changes made to their DNA. This is usually done by adding one or more genes to a species.

Currently the principle GMO foods out there are corn, soybeans, canola oil, cottonseed oil, and sugar from sugar beets. If it's labeled organic it shouldn't contain intentionally added GMO ingredients.

Apple grafting, which has been done since 2000 BC, is considered genetic altering , since it brings together 2 different varieties of apples. However, the grafting is done using an apple variety to another apple variety, not to a banana gene or a plum or a fish or a grasshopper gene. There is so much yet to be discovered about the safety of this process.

The risk here is that GM food has not been adequately identified and managed. GMO foods have been widespread without adequate knowledge of the dangers they present which may affect the health of consumers.

Use Healthy Cooking Oils

There has been a great deal of information and miss–information about what kind of oil to use. Again, it's important to use oils that have not been processed with unnecessary high heat and pressures. There should be an expiration date on oils.

Other standards to use when buying oils include:

no hydrogenation

no refining

no added chemicals

no bleaching

no GMO

certified organic

Here are the oils I feel are the healthiest and have been used in recipes requiring oil:

Butter, preferably made from the milk of grass–fed cattle

Coconut oil

Extra virgin olive oil

What you do today affects the way you look and feel. This includes:

the food you eat and how much you eat

how much you exercise and move

how much sleep you get

whether you get any sunshine

how much water you drink

Here I have concentrated mainly on working toward healthier practices through food. You need food for growth and to help you learn in school. Food is a friend to everyone. It's a matter of knowing what to eat and how much. The body is a wonderful mechanism. But it needs the proper fuel to do its job.

Working in the Kitchen

I want this cookbook to be the "go–to" apple recipe book for kids and teens. However, working with apples means there will be apples to peel, slice, chop, and otherwise prepare with a knife, if age appropriate.

Remember to keep safety precautions in mind when working in the kitchen. Pick up knives only by the handle and when you're through, lay the knife down flat on the counter. Small children may need to use only a butter or dinner knife.

When working with apples, always chop them on the cutting board, and not when you are holding the apple in your hand. Please use caution here when working with knives and other potentially dangerous pieces of equipment in the home. Very young children need to leave this job for an adult.

Other guidelines for working in the kitchen:

1. Always work with an adult, unless given permission by your parents or caregivers to work alone.

2. Read the recipe through and see that you have all the ingredients before you begin to cook.

3. Wash your hands before you begin.

4. Turn handles of pots and pans toward the center of the stove so they are not accidently knocked off.

5. Never plug in an appliance with wet hands.

6. Always use pot holders when handling hot dishes.

7. Know that stove top and oven are hot. Adults should cook foods on the stove top and place and remove food from the oven.

8. Use standard measuring cups and spoons.

9. Keep your work–top clean.

10. Do not lick your fingers or mixing spoons.

11. Please note that many of the recipes in this cookbook require adult assistance.

Apple Guide

The following is a guide to the varieties of apples you can use for different purposes. Again, climate and growing conditions can alter the flavor of any apple. You probably have some definite likes when it comes to choosing apples. Here are my favorite varieties to use for different purposes:

Apples for eating–in–hand and in salads

Braeburn

Fuji

Gala

Golden Delicious

Grimes Golden

HoneyCrisp

Red Delicious

Apples for cooking and making applesauce

Braeburn

Cortland

Harolson

Jonathan

Jonogold

Macoun

McIntosh

Northern Spy

Wealthy

Winesap

Apples for cooking in pies, tarts, crisps, and other desserts

Braeburn	Jonathan
Cortland	Jonogold
Gala	Macoun
Golden Delicious	Rome Beauty
Granny Smith	Wealthy
Grimes Golden	Winesap
Ida Red	

Note: buy organic, if possible. Peel apples that are not organic.

Note: If you are using drier than normal apples, use a bit more water or liquid in the baked recipes.

Cooking with apples is not always an exact science as the quality, degree of sweetness, and juiciness of the apples varies.

Drinks

Wassail (pronounced: 'wä–sæl, wä–'sãl)

Wassail is a hot drink traditionally served at Christmas. This goes back to ancient times when this ritual was intended to ask God for a good apple harvest the following year.

Ingredients
1 quart apple cider
2 cups cranberry juice
1 cup orange juice
1 teaspoon allspice
Pinch of nutmeg
2 apples
1 orange
1 teaspoon whole cloves
3 cinnamon sticks

Tools & Equipment
slow cooker or large pot
large spoon for stirring
cutting board
paring knife

1. In a slow–cooker or a large pot over low heat, combine apple cider and juices. Add allspice and nutmeg. Break cinnamon sticks in half and add. Bring to a simmer but do not boil.

2. Slice the oranges crosswise into ¼ inch slices but do not peel.

3. Carefully slice off the top of apples at stem end. Cut the core out of apples. Slice into rings about the thickness of bread slices. Poke whole cloves into orange and apples. Add to pot (they will float). If using a slow cooker, cook for 2–4 hours.

4. Serve hot.

Hot Spiced Cider for a Crowd

Keep this recipe in mind for Halloween. Hot apple cider really warms you up after a night of "Trick or Treating".

Ingredients
6 cups apple cider
  or 3 (46 ounce) cans
apple juice
3 sticks cinnamon
6 whole cloves

Tools & Equipment
30—cup coffee maker or
  large pan

1. Pour apple cider or juice into 30—cup coffee maker or large pan.
2. In coffee basket (or large pan) place cinnamon sticks, broken in pieces, and whole cloves.
3. Perk through cycle of automatic coffee maker or heat to simmering. Keep hot.

Appaloosa Alert

No, it's not horse related. Appaloosa horses are known for their beauty and performance. This apple drink alerts you to the sparkle and joy in your life.

Ingredients
½ cup apple juice
1 cup fresh orange juice
1 teaspoon honey
2 tablespoons nonfat
  dry milk
½ teaspoon vanilla
2 ice cubes

Tools & Equipment
blender
spoon
ice tongs
measuring spoons

1. Mix all in blender on high until ice is melted.

2. Pour into glasses and serve immediately.

Makes 2 cups

Fruity Smoothie

When choosing apple juice or apple cider, it's recommended to select shelf–stable, frozen or other fruit juices and ciders that have been pasteurized or appropriately heat–treated for safety.

Ingredients

1 cup apple juice
1 cup orange juice
½ apple, peeled and cut up
1 frozen banana, sliced or
  broken up
1 cup sliced fresh or frozen
  strawberries
½ cup instant nonfat dry milk powder
2 teaspoons honey

Tools & Equipment

blender
large pitcher
tall glasses

1. Place all ingredients in blender. Blend at high speed until smooth and creamy.
2. Pour into tall glasses and enjoy.

Makes about 4 glasses

Collection of Recipes for Juicing

Here is a large selection of drinks you can make if you have a juicer. It's amazing the combinations you can make using apples and other fruits or vegetables. This is MUCH better than buying fruity drinks at the store.

First wash fruits and vegetables in water with a little vinegar and salt added or use a non–toxic, biodegradable cleaner. Cut them into pieces small enough to fit into the feeder tube of your juicer. Use only the plunger provided with your juicer. Never push food into feeder with your fingers.

Sugar–Less Lemonade
4 apples (use peeled or unpeeled with seeds, stem, and core removed) cut into chunks
¼ lemon (with skin) cut into pieces

1. No water and no sugar are needed.
2. Just add crushed ice.

Apple/Carrot
2 apples (use peeled or unpeeled with seeds, stem, and core removed)
6 carrots (put large end first into feeder tube)

Apple/Carrot/Celery

6 carrots
1 apple
2 stalks of celery (push through slowly as fibers are tough)

Apple/Veggies

2 apples
handful of grapes
2 celery stalks
4 stalks kale
2 big carrots
2 handfuls of spinach

Apple/Strawberries

2 apples
4–6 strawberries

Apple/Grapefruit

1 apple
1 white or pink grapefruit (peeled)

Apple/Pineapple/Strawberries

1 Red Delicious apple
2 rings of pineapple
6 strawberries

Apples/Grapes/Lemon

2 apples
1 large bunch grapes
1–inch slice lemon with peel

Salads

Three-Fruit Salad

You can try apples, oranges, and avocados, or ? Be original! Be creative! My favorite way to serve a fruit salad is to cut up fruit, pour a little orange juice over it, and serve.

Ingredients
1 Delicious apple, unpeeled
1 banana
¼ cup pineapple chunks, unsweetened, drained

Tools & Equipment
paring knife
small bowl
measuring spoons

1. Wash apple. Halve, quarter, and cut in small pieces.

2. Peel banana and slice.

3. Combine fruits and serve with following:

Dressing
¼ cup plain yogurt
1–2 tablespoons unsweetened pineapple juice
⅛ teaspoon nutmeg

4. Blend ingredients and pour over fruit.

5. Serve fruit salad in dishes or on plates with bed of lettuce.

Yield: 4 servings

Note: Sliced apples turn brown when exposed to air. You can keep them from turning this unappetizing brown color by placing them in water with a few drops of fresh lemon. Then rinse them before serving. Any citrus juice works well, too, even pineapple juice. Another method is to place the sliced apples in cool salt water. Use about 1 tablespoon salt to a quart of water. After all the apples are sliced, rinse them in a strainer under cool running water. Store them in a sealed container until ready to use or serve. They will not end up turning brown.

Apple Waldorf Salad

This is a popular salad with a long history. The first Waldorf Salad was said to have been created in 1893 at the Waldorf Astoria hotel in New York City.

Ingredients
2 large apples, unpeeled
  and cut into small chunks
1 stalk chopped celery
¼ cup mayonnaise
Squeeze of lemon juice
Orange juice to desired consistency

Tools & Equipment
cutting board
paring knife
spoon

1. Prepare apples and celery.
2. Mix together mayonnaise and juices. When ready to serve, use only enough dressing to lightly coat apples and celery.

Serve on a lettuce leaf.

Coconut Fruit Salad

Apple season is a great time of year. Apples can be bought all year long, but September and October are truly considered the best months of the apple season.

Ingredients
2 apples, unpeeled
2 oranges
1 cup grapes
1 teaspoon honey
1 tablespoon cornstarch
1 cup apple juice or
  orange juice
½ cup coconut

Tools & Equipment
small saucepan
measuring cups and
  spoons
mixing spoon
cutting board
paring knife

1. In small saucepan, mix honey, cornstarch, and juice. Cook over medium heat until thickened, stirring to prevent scorching. Cool.

2. Prepare fruit. Add to cooled juice mixture. Stir lightly. Serve in individual dishes and sprinkle top with coconut.

Ambrosia Salad

"Ambrosia" refers to the 'food of the gods', something especially delicious to taste or smell. Other fruits can be included in this salad, such as berries (strawberries, raspberries, and blueberries), mandarin oranges, bananas, plums, kiwis, etc. The tasty dressing enhances the flavor of all.

Ingredients
1 orange
2 Delicious apples
Watermelon 1 cup, chunked
2 fresh peaches
1 tablespoon lemon juice
½ cup sour cream
1 teaspoon honey
¼ cup coconut

Tools & Equipment
cutting board
paring knife
small mixing bowl
measuring cups
spoons
rubber scraper

1. Wash the fruit. With a paring knife, cut off any peels and stems. Take out seeds.

2. On chopping board, cut up the fruit and pile into a bowl.

3. Drizzle lemon juice over apples and peaches to prevent them from turning brown.

4. Spoon sour cream into small mixing bowl. Mix honey and coconut into the sour cream.

5. Gently blend all together and serve immediately.

Note: If you will not serve the ambrosia right away, cover the fruit and the sour cream mixture separately and refrigerate until serving time.

Yield: 6 servings

Apple/Orange Salad with Feta

Feta is a variety of cheese that tastes extra special with apples. It is a type of Greek cheese that is brined or pickled. That is what gives it a slightly salty, tangy flavor. It tends to crumble easily, making it easy to add; although you can often find it already crumbled in the cheese section of the grocery store.

Ingredients

1 red apple, cored and sliced
3 oranges
6 cups mixed baby greens
3–4 tablespoons freshly
  squeezed orange juice
2 tablespoons extra–virgin olive oil
¼ teaspoon coarse salt
½ cup crumbled feta cheese

Tools & Equipment

cutting board
paring knife
grater
whisk or fork

1. Core and slice apple. Grate rind from 1 orange into a small bowl. Squeeze juice to equal 3–4 tablespoons. Peel and section oranges.

2. Combine apple, oranges, and greens.

3. Whisk together juice, olive oil, salt, and orange rind. Pour over salad and toss gently.

4. Spoon onto serving plates and sprinkle with crumbled cheese.

Serves 8

Chicken Apple Salad

Most any variety of apple will work in this salad. When choosing apples, look for those that are free from bruises, blemishes, and skin breaks. They should be firm with no soft spots or bruises, breaks in the skin, or insect damage.

Ingredients

I cup cooked chicken
I medium apple
I stalk celery
¼ cup walnuts
lettuce leaf
Drizzle of **Dressing**

Tools & Equipment

cutting board
paring knife
food processor, optional
measuring cup
medium bowl
spoon

1. On cutting board, cut chicken into small cubes. Place in medium bowl.

2. Wash apple; halve and quarter. Cut into small pieces.

3. Wash celery and cut into bite–size pieces.

4. Chop walnuts on cutting board or in food processor.

5. Combine chicken, apple, celery, and walnuts. Mix well.

6. Make dressing and serve on lettuce leaf.

Dressing

¼ cup extra–virgin olive oil   2 tablespoons vinegar
I teaspoon honey   I teaspoon Dijon mustard
I tablespoon snipped parsley
Salt and freshly ground black pepper to taste

Shake dressing ingredients in a covered container. Use only enough dressing to lightly coat salad.

Yield: 4 servings

Apple Macaroni Salad

Apples give this dish a nice "crunch". Store apples in their plastic bag in the crisper part of the refrigerator at close to 32 degrees. The freezing point of apples, which is damaging to the fruit, is about 28 or 29 degrees.

Ingredients

1 cup cooked and drained macaroni

2 Delicious apples or other as indicated on page 19

Lemon juice

½ cup celery, cut into bite–size pieces

4 green onions, chop whites and cut off green

¼ green pepper, chopped

1 tablespoon pimento, well drained and chopped

1 cup shredded sharp Cheddar cheese

½ cup mayonnaise

¼ teaspoon salt

½ teaspoon dry mustard

1 teaspoon balsamic vinegar

Tools & Equipment

cutting board

paring knife

large bowl

1. Wash, core, and chop apples into small chunks. Drizzle with lemon juice to keep from darkening.

2. In a large bowl, add apple, cooked macaroni, and vegetables.

3. Stir salt, mustard, and balsamic vinegar into mayonnaise. Spoon over salad and gently mix to combine. Sprinkle cheese over top.

4. Cover and chill at least 2 hours before serving.

Breads and Cereals

Granola with Apples and Other Goodies

You will find many different kinds of dried fruits in the grocery store, or you can make your own. See page 101 on making your own dried apples.

Ingredients

4 cups oatmeal (regular or quick)
2 tablespoons honey or
  pure maple syrup
½ cup (1 stick) butter, melted
½ cup walnuts
¼ teaspoon salt
½ teaspoon cinnamon
¼ – ½ teaspoon nutmeg

Extras to add, or omit:
½ cup dried apples, cut into chunks
¼ cup dried cranberries
½ cup chopped almonds
½ cup sunflower seeds
¼ teaspoon sesame seeds

Tools & Equipment

cookie sheet
parchment paper
small saucepan
large bowl
spoon
rubber scraper
long–handled spatula
parchment paper

1. Preheat oven to 350° F. Cover cookie sheet pan with parchment paper or foil.

2. In small saucepan, melt butter. Add honey or syrup to butter. Set aside.

3. Mix oatmeal, walnuts and seasonings in a large bowl.

4. Pour melted butter mixture over oatmeal and mix thoroughly.

5. Spread on parchment covered cookie sheet.

6. Bake for 15–20 minutes, checking and stirring every 10 minutes until flakes are a light golden brown. Rather go light than dark — burns easily.

7. Remove from oven. Mix in nuts and dried fruits. When cool, store in a large airtight container with a scoop inside.

Variation: Peanut Butter Granola: Mix in ¾ cup creamy peanut butter with butter and honey. Place oatmeal in a shallow roasting pan. Pour the peanut butter mixture over the oatmeal. Stir gently until all the oatmeal is coated.

Bake in 300° F oven for about 20 minutes *(watching to see that oatmeal doesn't brown too much and stirring occasionally)*. Turn off oven. Stir in any special ingredients as listed above. Let dry in the oven with the door closed for an hour, stirring occasionally.

Store in a covered container. I like to add a scoop for easy dishing out. Makes a great snack as well as hearty breakfast food.

Spiced Apple Oatmeal with Raisin Sauce

Wash apples just before using them, as their protective coating helps keep them from becoming shriveled and bruised. I generally peel apples for use, but in this recipe the apple is added to boiling water, so I feel you can either peel or not peel it.

Ingredients
1 cup water
1 cooking apple, cored & chopped (peel on or off)
½ cup quick cooking oatmeal
½ teaspoon cinnamon
½ teaspoon nutmeg

Tools & Equipment
2 small saucepans
mixing spoon
measuring spoon

1. Bring water to boil.
2. Adult needs to add oatmeal, chopped apple, and spices.
3. Lower heat and cook 2–3 minutes.

Raisin Sauce
1½ cups water
½ cup raisins
⅓ cup white grape juice, concentrate, thawed
1 tablespoon butter
1 teaspoon cornstarch

1. In small pan, add water and raisins and bring to a boil.
2. Add juice concentrate and simmer for 10 minutes.
3. Add butter and cornstarch and boil for 1 minute.
4. When desired consistency is reached, cool slightly and serve over oatmeal.

Yield: 2 servings of oatmeal, with enough sauce for another day.

Apple Walnut Muffins

This is your basic muffin recipe with added apples and walnuts. Eating fresh–from–the–oven muffins is a treat to be enjoyed often.

Ingredients

2 cups flour
¼ cup cane sugar
3 teaspoons baking powder
½ teaspoon salt
2 teaspoons cinnamon
3 tablespoons melted
  butter
1 egg
1 cup cider (or milk)
½ cup chopped walnuts
2 apples, such as Granny Smith, peeled, diced

Tools & Equipment

12–cup muffin pan
large mixing bowl
small mixing bowl
measuring cups
measuring spoons
mixing spoon
spatula
muffin liners, optional

1. Grease muffin pan or use muffin liners.

2. In a bowl mix together dry ingredients.

3. In a small bowl, beat together melted butter, egg, and cider (or milk).

4. Make a well in the center of dry ingredients and pour in the wet ingredients.

5. Add walnuts and diced apple.

6. Mix only until all ingredients are moistened. Don't over mix The batter should be lumpy.

7. Spoon into prepared pan and fill ⅔ full. Bake at 400° F 20–30 minutes or until the muffin tops are nicely browned.

Muffins freeze beautifully. To reheat frozen muffins, unwrap and microwave, or heat in oven at 350° F for 10 minutes or so. They're so easy to pop in and have for breakfast before school.

Good Morning Muffins

Can you guess what one ingredient looks out of place in this recipe? Yes, you guessed it — carrots. Carrots in muffins, you ask? Ah, it adds crunchiness plus nutrients — what more can you ask?

Ingredients

1 cup whole wheat flour
1 cup oat bran or rice flour
2 teaspoons baking powder
2 teaspoons cinnamon
¼ teaspoon nutmeg
¼ teaspoon salt
1 egg
½ cup oil
¼ cup honey
½ cup applesauce, unsweetened
2 teaspoons vanilla
2 cups chopped apples (peeled or unpeeled)
½ cup grated carrots (about 1 large carrot)
½ cups raisins
¼ cup chopped walnuts

Tools & Equipment

2, 12–cup muffin pans
muffin pan liners, optional
large mixing bowl
small mixing bowl
whisk or fork
mixing spoon

1. Preheat oven to 350° F. Grease muffin tins or line with paper inserts.

2. In large mixing bowl, mix together flours, baking powder, cinnamon, nutmeg, and salt.

3. In a separate bowl, whisk together egg, oil, honey, applesauce, and vanilla. Add to flour mixture and stir

just until mixture is moistened. Stir in apples, carrots, raisins and walnuts and stir to blend.

4. Spoon batter into 18 muffin tins. Fill each about ⅔ full.

5. Bake for 20 minutes or until a toothpick inserted in center comes out clean.

Makes: 24 muffins

Applesauce Muffins

Applesauce is so easy to make Just peel, core, and quarter however many apples you want, add a little water, cook until tender, then add cinnamon to taste. You don't need all that sugar often found in recipes. Try it.

Ingredients

1¼ cups applesauce, unsweetened
¼ cup honey
2 tablespoons oil
1 large egg
1 teaspoon vanilla
2 cups flour
2 teaspoons baking powder
½ teaspoon soda
½ teaspoon salt
½ teaspoon cinnamon
¼ teaspoon nutmeg
½ cup raisins
½ cup nuts

Tools & Equipment

12–cup muffin pan
muffin pan liners
  optional
medium sized bowl
mixing spoon
measuring cups
measuring spoons
rubber scraper

1. Preheat oven to 350° F. Grease muffin pan or insert paper liners in pan.

2. In medium–sized mixing bowl, add applesauce, honey, and oil. Mix in egg and vanilla.

3. Add dry ingredients, raisins, and nuts.

4. Mix together just until all ingredients are moistened.

5. Spoon in batter until each cup is full.

6. Bake for 20–25 minutes or until lightly browned and toothpick inserted in center comes out clean.

Makes: 12 muffins

Apple Breakfast Granola Bars

No need to buy granola bars in the store. Just whip up a batch yourself using ingredients commonly found in the kitchen. You won't find any preservatives here.

Ingredients

1 large apple, peeled & chopped

1½ cups oatmeal

¼ cup flour

1 teaspoon cinnamon

⅓ cup honey

3 tablespoons oil

1 teaspoon vanilla

¼ teaspoon almond extract

¼ cup finely chopped almonds

Tools & Equipment

8 x 8–inch pan

cutting board

paring knife

small bowl

large mixing bowl

measuring cups and spoons

mixing spoon

1. Grease an 8 x 8–inch pan.

2. Peel and chop apple in small bowl.

3. Combine dry ingredients in a large bowl.

4. Measure honey in measuring cup and add in oil, vanilla, and almond extract. Add this to dry ingredients. Mix until all are moistened.

5. Mix in apples and almonds.

6. Press into prepared pan. You may need to wet your hands or use a damp spoon to press into place.

7. Bake at 350° F for 12–15 minutes. Remove from oven and cut into bars. Separate bars slightly and return to oven for 3–6 minutes more. There may be crumbling, but use those for snacks.

Apple Biscuit Coffee Cake

This is one of only a handful of recipes here that uses a prepared product – in this case, refrigerated buttermilk biscuits. This recipe is very easy to make and kids love making it and eating the "fruit" of their labor.

Ingredients

1 package (8–10) refrigerated buttermilk biscuits
2 tablespoons melted butter
2 large cooking apples, peeled, cored, and sliced
½ teaspoon cinnamon
¼ cup raisins
1 cup water
1 tablespoon honey
1 stick butter
½ teaspoon cinnamon
½ teaspoon vanilla
¼ cup walnuts

Tools & Equipment

9 x 9–inch pan
cutting board
paring knife
measuring spoons

1. Melt 2 tablespoons butter in bottom of baking pan.

2. Arrange sliced apples over butter. Sprinkle cinnamon and raisins over apples. Cut each biscuit into fourths and place over apple mixture.

3. In medium saucepan, add water, honey, butter, and cinnamon. Bring to a boil. Add vanilla.

4. Pour the hot mixture over the apples/biscuits. Sprinkle walnuts over top.

5. Bake in 350° F oven for 30–35 minutes or until golden brown.

Serve warm.

Makes: 6–8 servings

Apple Foldovers

Pancakes puff up and then deflate — don't panic! Good for breakfast as a glorified pancake or as a delectable dessert.

Ingredients
3–4 tart apples
2 tablespoons butter
2 tablespoons honey
½ teaspoon cinnamon
¼ teaspoon nutmeg

Tools & Equipment
cutting board
paring knife

1. Prepare apple filling by peeling apples and slicing them thin.
2. In 10–inch ovenproof skillet, sauté apples for 5 minutes in butter until they are tender crisp.
3. Add honey and spices. Cover and continue cooking for 10 minutes. Spoon apple filling into another dish.

Batter
3 eggs
¾ cup flour
¼ teaspoon salt
¾ cup milk
1 tablespoon butter
1 teaspoon vanilla
Dash of cinnamon

egg beater
mixing bowl
measuring cup
10–inch skillet

1. Heat oven to 425° F.

2. Using the same non–stick oven proof 10–inch skillet you used for the apples, melt butter in pan in oven.

3. In blender or with egg beater, beat 3 eggs. Add flour, salt, and milk alternately while eggs are blending or beating. Add vanilla; blend 1 minute.

4. Pour into heated skillet with melted butter. Sprinkle top of mixture with cinnamon to taste.

5. Bake at 425° F for 20 minutes. Remove from oven. Spread apple filling over one–half of the mixture. Fold over. Place on serving plate and slice.

Serve hot.

Makes 4 – 6 servings.

Apple Pancakes

Use Granny Smith apples for a hint of tartness or sweeter varieties such as Gala, Braeburn, or Delicious. Your mornings will never be the same after you try this recipe! Gone are the "dry cereal with milk" days.

Ingredients

1½ cups flour
2 teaspoons baking powder
Pinch of salt
2 eggs, beaten
1 cup milk
2 tablespoons butter, melted
1 apple, peeled and grated
1–3 tablespoons butter for pan or griddle

Tools & Equipment

medium size bowl or large measuring pitcher
measuring cup and spoons
paring knife
pan or griddle
mixing spoon
rubber scraper
spatula
cutting board
grater or food processor

1. Combine dry ingredients in one bowl. In a separate bowl, beat eggs; add milk, melted butter, and grated apple. Stir only until dry ingredients are moistened.

2. Heat pan or griddle over medium heat. Add remaining butter to pan. Add the batter by heaping tablespoon and cook until bubbles begin to appear on top. Then flip and cook until bottom is nicely browned.

Serve with warm applesauce or "real" maple syrup.

Spiced Apple Loaf

This recipe makes 3 loaves. You can give one to a friend. I like this saying about a friend: "There are some people in life who make you laugh a little louder, smile a little bigger, and just live a little better."

Ingredients

3 cups flour
2 teaspoons baking powder
¼ teaspoon baking soda
½ teaspoon salt
1 teaspoon cinnamon
½ teaspoon nutmeg
¼ to ½ cup cane sugar
3 eggs
½ cup oil
¾ cup sour milk
2 cups apples, peeled and grated
½ cup chopped nuts
1 teaspoon vanilla

Tools & Equipment

large mixing bowl
measuring cups &
  spoons
mixing spoon
rubber scraper
cutting board
paring knife
3, 8 x 4 x 2–inch loaf
  pans

1. In large mixing bowl, add the dry ingredients and mix together. Make a well in the center.

2. To this, add eggs, oil, and sour milk. Mix well.

Note: to make sour milk, pour ¾ cup milk into measuring cup and add 1½ teaspoon vinegar or lemon juice. Let it set a few minutes and add to mixture.

3. Blend in apples, nuts, and vanilla.

4. Pour batter into greased loaf pans and bake at 325° F for 45 minutes or until a toothpick inserted in center comes out clean. Let cool for 15 minutes, then remove from pans and cool on rack.

Breakfast Oatmeal Treats

Apples come in different forms, such as in juice, raw, and dried. Apples also come in different shades of reds, yellow, and greens. Choose clear colored apples. Often those with an intense green undercast or undertone are not completely ripe. Those with a dull yellowish–green undercast may be too ripe.

Ingredients

2 cups oatmeal
¼ teaspoon salt
⅓ cup cane sugar
1 teaspoon baking powder
1 teaspoon cinnamon
¼ cup oil
1 large egg
¾ cup milk
½ cup dried apples, chopped
½ cup raisins
½ cup nuts, chopped

Tools and Equipment

large mixing bowl
mixing spoon & fork
measuring cup & spoons
small bowl
9 x 9–inch pan

1. Grease a 9 x 9–inch pan.
2. Measure oatmeal, salt, cane sugar, baking powder, and cinnamon in large mixing bowl.
3. Crack egg into small bowl and stir with fork.
4. Add egg and milk to dry ingredients. Stir until well blended.
5. Add dried apples, raisins, and nuts. Stir to combine.
6. Scrape into prepared pan. Bake at 350° F for 30 minutes. Cut while still slightly warm.

Makes 9 squares

Sandwiches

Apple-Witches

These "sandwiches" are made with apple slices instead of bread slices. When shopping for apples, do you naturally reach for the largest apple? The biggest is not always the best. Big costs more. The bigger the apple the quicker it matured and the more likely firmness and texture are on the way out.

Ingredients
Apples
Orange or lemon juice

Tools & Equipment
cutting board
paring knife
small bowl for juice

Fillings such as:
Peanut butter
Peanut butter and banana
Peanut butter and jelly
Cream cheese
Cheese spread
Tuna salad

1. Wash and core apples.
2. Carefully slice off the top of apples at stem end.
3. Slice apples into rings about the thickness of bread slices.
4. Dip slices into orange or lemon juice to prevent browning.
5. Spread any of the fillings on an apple slice. Top with another apple ring if filling allows it. Munch away!

Apple Grilled-Cheese Sandwiches

Did you know that apples are living, breathing organisms? The apple you ate today won't taste or smell or feel quite the same as it would have yesterday or tomorrow. They are always changing. Even in the refrigerator their life cycle continues after harvest.

Ingredients
4 slices raisin bread
1 apple
4 slices (4 ounce) Cheddar cheese
1 tablespoon butter, softened

Tools & Equipment
cutting board
paring knife
frying pan or griddle
spatula

1. Wash, core, and thinly slice apple.
2. Spread softened butter on one side of each slice of bread.
3. Place 4 bread slices, butter side down, in frying pan or griddle. (An electric skillet works well).
4. Place a Cheddar cheese slice on each slice of bread and cover with apple slices.
5. Place second piece of bread on top, buttered side up.
6. Cook over medium heat until bottom is golden brown.
7. Turn over and cook until other side of bread is browned and cheese is melted.

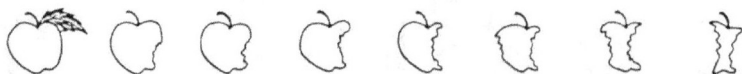

Yummy Apple Sandwich

Spread apple butter on any of the following:

Whole wheat bread or toast
English muffins
Whole grain bagels
Pita bread

Add raisins or slice of cheese, if desired

Apple-Peanut Butter Sandwiches

John Chapman, better known as Johnny Appleseed has become a fixture in American folklore. He was born in Massachusetts during the Revolutionary War. He is known for planting apples throughout the eastern part of the United States. His style of living made him a memorable character. It was said he slept in a tree–top hammock, that he had a pet wolf, and that he played with a bear family. He was a friend to all animals and to the settlers moving west. We often see pictures of him with a pot on his head, which answered both as a cap and as a cooking utensil.

Ingredients

Whole wheat bread (or
   other firm–textured bread)
Peanut butter
1 apple
1 banana

Tools & Equipment

butter knife
cutting board
paring knife

1. Spread peanut butter on one side of bread.

2. Cut slices into fourths.

3. Peel and slice banana.

4. Wash, core, and slice apple. Arrange apple and banana slices on each quarter bread.

A variation of this is to spread each slice with cream cheese that has been softened and mixed with a few tablespoons of milk to give it a good spreading consistency. Top with apple slices, banana slices, and raisins. Add chopped nuts, if desired.

Apple-Peanut Butter Roll-Ups

A fun, after—school snack! Fun apple sayings include:

You're the apple of my eye.
He knows how to polish the apple!
Don't upset the apple cart.
The apple never falls far from the tree.
One rotten apple spoils the whole bunch.
An apple a day keeps the doctor away.

Ingredients

1 apple
Bread, whole wheat
  or other
Peanut butter

Tools & Equipment

cutting board
paring knife
rolling pin
grater

1. Wash, core, and peel apple. Flatten slice of bread with rolling pin.

2. Spread peanut butter on bread. Grate fresh apple on top.

3. Roll each slice up like a jelly roll. Seal roll with peanut butter.

4. Cut into slices.

Main Dishes

Slow Cooker Beef Roast with Apples and Veggies

Growing an apple tree and getting apples from the tree is a long, slow process. Apples take three to ten years for the seedlings to grow up and bear fruit. The wonderful thing about apple trees is they can be enjoyed by almost anyone willing to invest time, energy, and patience into growing them.

Ingredients

3–4 pound beef roast
  (chuck, round, rump, etc.).
1 tablespoon olive oil
1½ teaspoons salt
⅛ teaspoon pepper
1 large onion, cut in half, then chunk into quarters
3 large red apples, skin on, cored and cut into quarters
½ pound baby carrots or trimmed carrots, peeled
4 whole cloves
½ teaspoon ginger
2 cups apple cider or juice
3–4 tablespoons flour
3–4 tablespoons water

Tools & Equipment

slow cooker
measuring cup & spoons
cutting board
paring knife

1. Lightly grease inside of slow cooker. Place prepared onion and apples in bottom of cooker.

2. Rinse meat under cool water, then place on top of onions and apples. (Cut meat in half or smaller sections if needed to fit well into cooker). Lightly rub olive oil all over meat. Sprinkle liberally with seasonings. Poke whole cloves into the meat.

3. Pour apple cider or juice around the meat.

4. Cover and cook on HIGH for 6–8 hours or LOW for 10–12 hours until tender. About halfway through the cooking, add the carrots.

5. In a container with a tight–fitting lid, put 3–4 tablespoons of flour and enough water to make the consistency of a paste. Shake the daylights out of it and gradually whisk it into the broth to thicken it. Put the lid back on meat and allow the roast to cook for about 30 more minutes, or until the sauce has thickened. Stir occasionally.

6. Pour gravy and carrots over roast when serving. The onion and apples will be very mushy and can be served as sauce with the meat, if desired.

Orchardists have been busy developing just the "right" apple for hundreds of years. Perhaps the most notable is the history of the Red Delicious apple. Stark Nurseries of Louisiana, Missouri, sponsored an Apple Show and Contest in 1892. Growers brought their best fruit to the show. In the testing process, Clarence Stark bit into a red, rather elongated apple with five small bumps on the blossom end, and exclaimed, "Delicious! Who sent them?" However, the grower could not be found. The next year another contest was sponsored, in the hopes of again finding the best apple. This time the apple grower was identified. The tree bearing the extra–ordinary red apple came from the farm of Jesse Hiatt of Winterset, Iowa. Stark purchased its sole rights, named the apple "Stark Delicious," and secured a registered trade mark. It has become the world's most popular and profitable apple.

Main Dishes   63

Meat Loaf with Zesty Topping

Applesauce keeps this meat loaf nice and moist. What's the difference between applesauce and apple butter you ask? Apple butter is cooked down more so it's thicker and often has spices and sweetening added.

Ingredients

1½ pounds ground beef
¼ medium onion, minced
2 slices dry toast, cubed
¾ cup applesauce, unsweetened
1 teaspoon salt
¼ teaspoon pepper

Tools & Equipment

9 x 5 x 3–inch loaf pan
large mixing bowl
cutting board
paring knife for onion
measuring spoons
mixing spoon
small mixing bowl

Topping

2 tablespoons catsup
1 teaspoon dry mustard
1 teaspoon prepared horseradish

1. Mix together thoroughly ground beef, onions, dry bread cubes, applesauce and seasonings.
2. Pack into 9 x 5 x 3–inch greased loaf pan.
3. In small bowl, combine *Topping*. Mix catsup, mustard, and horseradish; spoon over top of loaf.
4. Bake at 325° F for 1 hour.

Serves: 6

Ham and Apples

Duchess and Wealthy were apple varieties recommended on the list in 1889. The apple variety, Gem City, was a seedling discovered in Wisconsin before 1905 and grown in Baraboo, Wisconsin. McIntosh was a seedling discovered on a farm in Ontario, Canada and introduced to the USA in 1907.

Ingredients

1 ham slice, ¾–inch thick
2 tart cooking apples,
  peeled
⅛ teaspoon cinnamon
⅛ teaspoon nutmeg
½ cup water

Tools & Equipment

cutting board
paring knife
measuring spoons

1. Brown ham slightly on both sides in fry pan. Slash fat on ham to prevent curling.

2. Place apple slices or rings over ham. Sprinkle with cinnamon and nutmeg. Pour water in pan and cover.

3. Cook until ham is browned nicely on the bottom.

Honey/Mustard Chicken and Apples

Luther Burbank was an early plant pioneer. He added a wealth of knowledge about fruit growing and left a legacy of rare hybrids, trees, and plants.

Ingredients

4 skinless, boneless chicken breasts
  breasts
3 tablespoons flour
½ teaspoon salt
¼ teaspoon pepper
2 tablespoons olive oil
2 cooking apples
½ cup apple cider
½ cup chicken broth
1½ teaspoons cornstarch
2 teaspoons honey
2 tablespoons Dijon mustard

Tools & Equipment

plate or wax paper
skillet
cutting board
paring knife
whisk
small bowl
measuring cup and
  spoons

1. On plate or wax paper, mix together flour, salt and pepper. Dredge the chicken in flour (roll chicken in flour) and shake off the excess.

2. Heat oil in skillet over medium heat. Add chicken and brown on both sides, about 6 minutes on each side or until center is cooked.

3. Core apples, cut into eighths, and add to chicken.

4. Meanwhile, whisk cider, chicken broth, cornstarch, honey, and mustard in a bowl.

5. Add this to chicken/apples and bring to a boil. Turn heat down to low, cover pot and simmer until chicken is tender, about 15 minutes.

6. To serve, spoon sauce over chicken and apples.

Serves: 4

Side Dishes

Sautéed Apples

Good to serve with ham, sausage, or pork. Really easy to make and is good on it's own as well. Any of these apples work well: Rome, Jonagold, Granny Smith, Pippin, Gala, Braeburn, Northern Spy, Gravenstein, Rhode Island Greening, York Imperial, and Cortland.

Ingredients

2 teaspoons butter
2 firm, tart apples, peeled, cored and sliced ¼ inch thick
Pinch of cinnamon, if desired

Tools & Equipment

skillet or saucepan
cutting board
paring knife

1. In a large skillet or saucepan, melt butter over medium heat; add apples.
2. Cook, stirring constantly, until apples are almost tender (about 5–7 minutes).

Serves: 4

Baked Apples

I like this quote attributed to Martin Luther:
"Even if I knew that tomorrow the world would go to pieces,
I would still plant my apple tree." May we continue to plant
trees and never run out of apples!

Ingredients
4 cooking apples
2 teaspoons honey, or less
¼ teaspoon cinnamon
⅛ teaspoon nutmeg
2 teaspoons butter
½ cup water

Tools & Equipment
8 x 11–inch pan
measuring cup and spoons
cutting board
paring knife

1. Core apples, but not all the way through.
2. Place apples in 8 x 11–inch baking pan. In each cavity, put ½ teaspoon (or less) of honey and sprinkle with spices.
3. Top with butter. Pour water around apples.
4. Bake at 350° F for 30–40 minutes or until apples are tender but still hold their shape.

Makes: 4 servings

Apple-Yam Bake

The orchards of America have produced well over a thousand varieties of apples. People have come up with all kinds of different ways to use apples. Here is another interesting combination:

Ingredients

2 cooking apples, cored and sliced
1 can (17 ounces) whole yams
2 tablespoons frozen orange juice
  concentrate, thawed
1 tablespoon lemon juice
½ tablespoon butter
Ground cinnamon
Ground ginger

Tools & Equipment

cutting board
paring knife
casserole dish
can opener
measuring spoons

1. Grease shallow casserole. Place apples and yams in casserole; drizzle with orange juice concentrate and lemon juice. Dot with butter.

2. Sprinkle cinnamon and ginger overall.

3. Cover and bake at 325° F for 20 minutes or until apples are tender and yams are heated through.

Makes: 6 servings

Stuffing with Honeycrisp Apples

The Honeycrisp variety is a "new kid on the block". It was developed by the University of Minnesota and introduced in 1991. Some believe it to be the best, most exciting apple ever introduced.

Ingredients

1 stick butter
1 large onion, chopped
About 6 ribs of celery, chopped
1 teaspoon dried sage
1 teaspoon salt
¼ teaspoon black pepper
14 oz. bag seasoned stuffing
3 medium Honey Crisp apples, diced
3 cups chicken broth

Tools & Equipment

medium skillet
large roaster or 9 x 13 inch baking pan
paring knife

1. Melt butter in a medium skillet. Add onion and celery; sauté until tender. Add sage, salt, and pepper.

2. Place bread in large roaster or large bowl. Add onion mixture, apples, and broth; toss well to combine.

3. If using roaster, bake in 375° F oven for 20 minutes, otherwise, transfer stuffing to a 9 x 13–inch baking pan and bake for 20 minutes. Remove from oven and stir. If stuffing is too dry, add more broth.

4. Return to oven and bake 15 minutes.

Serves 10

Cakes

Applesauce Cake

Here's a little apple—mania: Did you know you can soften brown sugar with apples? All you have to do is place an apple wedge in the self—sealing plastic bag with the chunk of hardened brown sugar. Then you seal it up tightly and put it in a dry place for a day or two. The sugar will once again be soft enough to use. Remember to take out the apple.

Ingredients

1 cup flour
1 teaspoon baking powder
½ teaspoons baking soda
½ teaspoon cinnamon
½ teaspoon cloves
¼ teaspoon nutmeg
¼ teaspoon salt
1 egg
½ cup oil
½ cup cane sugar
1 cup applesauce, unsweetened
½ cup raisins

Tools & Equipment

8 x 8—inch baking pan
small mixing bowl
medium mixing bowl
measuring cups and spoons
mixing spoon
rubber scraper

1. Preheat oven to 300° F. Grease an 8 x 8—inch baking pan.

2. In a small mixing bowl, mix together flour, baking powder, baking soda, spices, and salt. Set aside.

3. In medium bowl, beat egg with fork; add oil, cane sugar, and applesauce. Add dry ingredients from small bowl and beat well by hand for 2 minutes.

4. Pour into greased pan and bake for 40 minutes at 300° F or until a toothpick inserted in the center comes out clean.

5. Serve warm with the following *Sauce* or *Maple Glaze*.

Sauce

⅓ cup cane sugar
1 tablespoon cornstarch
1 cup water
3 tablespoons butter
1 teaspoon vanilla

In saucepan, blend cornstarch with cane sugar. Add water. Cook over medium heat until thick and clear. Remove from heat; add butter and vanilla. Serve over baked cake.

Or, use this:

Maple Glaze

½ cup maple syrup
½ cup water
½ teaspoon vanilla
Pinch of salt

In saucepan over medium heat, combine all ingredients. Bring to a boil, then remove from heat and let cool.

Chunky Apple Cake

Jonathans and Winesaps are good all—around apples. Jonathans are an old variety and are famous for their flavor. Both are sweet and firm and make excellent cooking or baking apples .These varieties, as well as Granny Smith, which has a crisp, sharp, tart flavor, work well for this.

Ingredients

1 cup flour
1 teaspoon baking powder
½ teaspoon cinnamon
¼ teaspoon nutmeg
¼ teaspoon salt
¼ cup butter
½ cup cane sugar
  or ¼ cup honey
1 egg
1 teaspoon vanilla
2 medium tart apples,
  peeled and chopped
½ cup chopped walnuts
Whipping cream
1 teaspoon honey

Tools & Equipment

8 x 8—inch baking pan
small mixing bowl
small saucepan
large mixing bowl
mixing cups and spoons
mixing spoon
rubber scraper
cutting board
paring knife
food processor (optional)

1. Prepare apples. In small mixing bowl, combine flour, baking powder, cinnamon, nutmeg, and salt. Set aside.

2. Melt butter in small saucepan or microwave. Pour into large bowl. Add cane sugar or honey, egg, and vanilla. Beat well. Gradually add dry ingredients from small

bowl and beat well for 2 minutes. Stir in apples and walnuts.

3. Pour into greased baking pan and bake at 350° F for 35–40 minutes or until a toothpick inserted near the center comes out clean.

4. Whip the cream with 1 teaspoon of honey. Serve over cake.

"3 Kinds of Apples" Cake

An idea for a fun time with friends — host an apple tasting party. Buy different varieties of apples, cut them up in pieces so everyone can have a sample and try to guess what variety it is. Give your guests a list of the varieties you have on hand. You can also try to find out which is the sweetest, the most sour, the best tasting apple. You can pair this activity with cheese, or you can then serve this cake with an apple drink.

Ingredients

2 cups dried apples or
  mixture of fruit
2 apples, peeled and
chopped
¼ cup apple juice
  concentrate
½ cup oil
2 eggs, slightly beaten
1 teaspoon vanilla
2 cups flour
1 teaspoon baking powder
½ teaspoon baking soda
2 teaspoons cinnamon
½ teaspoon nutmeg
¼ teaspoon salt

Tools & Equipment

9 x 12–inch baking pan
medium saucepan
small & large mixing
  bowls
measuring cups and
  spoons
egg beater or mixer
mixing spoon
rubber scraper
food processor (optional)

1. In medium saucepan, add dried apples or mixed fruit and cover with water. Boil gently until all water is absorbed. *Watch so as not to let the water boil out completely!* Cool.

2. Beat eggs in small bowl.

3. Chop apples in large bowl. Add apple concentrate, oil, slightly beaten eggs, and vanilla. Mix to combine.

4. Add flour, baking powder, baking soda, spices, and salt. Mix well.

5. Fold in the cooled fruit mixture. Spoon into greased 9 x 12-inch baking pan.

6. Bake at 325° F for about 40–45 minutes.

Apple Filled Cake

Many exceptional varieties have come from abroad, such as Fuji and Mutsu from Japan and Braeburn and Southern Rose from New Zealand. Many native varieties have full flavor and a distinct richness all their own, such as Winesap, Cortland, Melrose, and Grimes Golden. The savvy apple lover will taste-test lots of different varieties.

Ingredients

4 apples, cored, peeled, quartered,
   sliced and cut into small chunks
½ cup flour
2 tablespoons cane sugar
1 teaspoon baking powder
⅛ teaspoon salt
2 eggs, slightly beaten
2 tablespoons oil
⅓ cup milk
1 teaspoon vanilla

Tools & Equipment

9–inch springform pan
small bowl or
waxed paper
medium bowl
measuring cups and
   spoons
mixing spoon
rubber scraper
cutting board
paring knife

Topping:

1 egg, slightly beaten
¼ cup cane sugar
1 teaspoon cinnamon
3 tablespoons butter, melted
¼ cup chopped nuts

1. Preheat oven to 400° F. Grease a 9–inch springform pan.

2. Prepare apples.

3. Measure dry ingredients in small bowl.

4. In medium size mixing bowl, beat eggs slightly, add oil, milk, and vanilla.

5. Add dry ingredients and stir until well–blended.

6. Mix in apples and stir well to thoroughly coat them with the batter. Spoon into prepared pan.

7. Bake about 25 minutes until fairly firm and golden.

Meanwhile, prepare the Topping:

1. In small bowl, combine the egg, cane sugar, cinnamon, melted butter, and nuts. Stir to blend. Set aside.

2. When cake is baked, remove from oven and pour topping mixture over it.

3. Return to oven and bake another 10 minutes or until the cake feels quite firm when pressed with the finger.

4. Run knife around sides of pan and release the springform but leave on the pan base.

5. Cut into thin wedges.

Bundt Apple Cake

A "bundt cake" is a cake baked in a bundt pan, which is round with fluted or grooved sides and a tube or chimney in the middle. The heat goes up the middle to help in more uniform baking. The pan needs to be well greased so the cake comes out of the pan easily without breaking up in a thousand pieces.

Ingredients

3 medium apples, peeled and
  chopped into small chunks
2 cups flour
¼ to ½ cup cane sugar
2½ teaspoons baking powder
1 teaspoon cinnamon
½ teaspoon salt
1 egg
¼ cup oil
1 cup milk
½ teaspoon vanilla

Tools & Equipment

Bundt cake pan
cutting board
paring knife
large mixing bowl
small mixing bowl
measuring cups
  and spoons
mixing spoon
food processor
  (optional)
fork

1. Grease a Bundt cake pan very well so cake won't stick.

2. Peel and chop apples.

3. In a large bowl, combine all the dry ingredients.

4. In a small bowl, beat egg slightly with fork, add milk and oil. Add to dry ingredients and stir until combined.

5. Place a layer of chopped apples in cake pan. Add remaining apples to the cake batter and stir to combine.

6. Spoon into pan and bake at 375° F for 40–45 minutes or until a toothpick comes out clean.

7. Let cool for 15 minutes and then gently loosen the outside of cake and the inner tube with a knife or a pliable spatula. Place plate over cake (use potholders!) and turn over to unmold. **An adult must do this!**

Serve warm or cold.

Refrigerator Fruit Cake

*Even very young children can help crush graham crackers
with a rolling pin. Many will be able to cut the dried apples
or other fruit into small pieces with scissors. This will be a real
help to the cook.*

Ingredients

4 cups graham cracker crumbs
1 teaspoon cinnamon
1 teaspoon nutmeg
2 cups dried apples or
mixture of fruit
¼ cup dates
1 cup chopped nuts
⅔ cup evaporated milk
½ cup frozen orange juice
concentrate

Tools & Equipment

2, 8–inch pans or
1, 9 x 12–inch pan
waxed paper
rolling pin
large mixing bowl
small mixing bowl
measuring cups
 and spoons
scissors for cutting
dried fruit

1. Prepare pans by lining with wax paper.

2. Between 2 sheets of waxed paper, crush graham
   crackers into crumbs with rolling pin (*or use food
   processor, if age permits*). Add to large bowl. Sprinkle in
   cinnamon and nutmeg. Add fruits and nuts.

3. Mix together evaporated milk and orange juice
   concentrate. Pour over crumb mixture and mix until all
   is moistened.

4. Place in prepared pans and pack firmly with hands.

5. Chill in refrigerator for 24 hours. Cut into small
   squares.

Pies

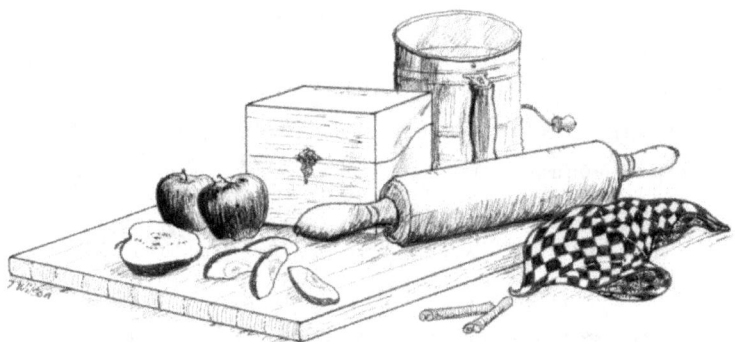

Mini Apple Pies

Visit orchards or roadside stands in your area. You may be pleasantly surprised at the wide variety of products they carry. There may be tubs of colorful mums and other flowers. Some sell fresh baked pies, cakes, and breads. Products such as apple cookbooks, apple peelers, and other apple collectibles appeal to orchard customers and others.

Ingredients

1 tube (8 oz.) refrigerated crescent rolls
1 cooking apple (such as Braeburn, Granny Smith, McIntosh, Jonathan)
6 tablespoons applesauce, unsweetened
½ teaspoon cinnamon

Tools & Equipment

6–7 muffin tins or custard cups
cutting board
paring knife
measuring spoons
rolling pin
3–inch round cookie cutter

1. Preheat oven to 400° F. Grease 6–7 muffin tins or custard cups.

2. Unroll crescent rolls and separate into two rectangles. Pinch the perforations together or roll with rolling pin to seal.

3. With a 3–inch round cookie cutter, cut 3 circles from each rectangle. Press dough into each of 6 muffin cups or custard cups. Collect left–over dough from cutouts and shape into circle for another cup or bake separately.

4. Peel, core, and thinly slice the apple. Place the slices, evenly divided, into the dough–lined cups. Cover with applesauce. Sprinkle cinnamon over applesauce.

5. Bake for 15–20 minutes.

Makes: 6–7 servings

Yummy Apple Pie Without Sugar

This does take time to peel, core, and slice about 6 to 8 apples. An apple peeler really helps when you're dealing with lots of apples. The finished product here is wonderful, just oozing with apples, and has NO added sugar.

Ingredients
Pastry for 2 crust 9–inch pie

Tools & Equipment
9–inch pie pan
large mixing bowl
  for apples
cutting board
paring knife

Filling
6 cups apples, peeled,
  cored, and sliced
1 (6 ounce) frozen apple juice
  concentrate, undiluted,
  unsweetened, thawed
2 tablespoons flour
1 teaspoon cinnamon
½ teaspoon nutmeg

3 quart saucepan
measuring spoons
rubber scraper
jar with tight
  fitting lid

1. In jar with tight–fitting lid, add thawed juice, flour, cinnamon, and nutmeg. Secure lid and shake jar until well blended.

2. Pour into 3 quart saucepan. Cook over medium heat, stirring constantly until mixture boils and thickens. Remove from heat.

3. Add apples to hot mixture. Stir until coated. Spoon into prepared pie shell. Add top crust and make slits in crust to allow steam to escape.

4. Bake at 425° F for 15 minutes, then reduce heat to 350° F and continue baking for 30–35 minutes or until crust is lightly browned and apples are tender. Cool on rack.

Serves: 6–8 slices

No Sugar Apple Pie

I have a little plastic apple peeler with a suction cup that grabs on to my counter top and I'm in business. I wouldn't give it up, even though there are larger, more impressive looking ones on the market. You just push on an apple, it pushes off when finished, and you end up with almost one long line of un–interrupted peeling. That's supposed to mean good luck, right?

Ingredients

1 2–crust, 9–inch pie crust
6–8 apples, peeled and sliced
¼ cup apple cider
1 tablespoon cinnamon

Tools & Equipment

pie pan
cutting board
paring knife
measuring spoons
fork

1. Mix apples, cider, and cinnamon.

2. Put into prepared pie shell.

3. Cover with top crust.

4. Brush on an egg glaze (1 egg beaten with 2 teaspoons of water).

5. Bake at 350° F for 50–60 minutes or until apples are tender.

More about apple peelers: An apple peeler/slicer is even more convenient. It's super fast and makes a bunch of apple rings in just minutes! Some attach to the edge of the counter and others have a suction base on them.

Cookies

Apple Oatmeal Cookies

The apple is probably the oldest fruit known to man. Whether Eve was tempted in the Garden of Eden with an apple, or a fig, or a mango, persimmon, or an apricot, is debatable. However, it has been found that prehistoric man ate apples and dried them, as noted by the charred remains of apples found in Stone Age lake dwellings in central Europe.

Ingredients

1 cup flour
1 cup oatmeal (regular or quick)
1 teaspoon baking powder
1 teaspoon cinnamon
¼ teaspoon salt
¼ cup water or apple juice
⅓ cup dried apples
⅓ cup raisins
2 eggs
⅓ cup oil
1 cup applesauce, unsweetened
¾ teaspoon vanilla
⅓ cup chopped nuts, optional

Tools & Equipment

cookie sheet
parchment paper
  (optional)
large mixing bowl
small saucepan
measuring cups
  and spoons
mixing spoon
rubber scraper

1. Grease cookie sheet or use parchment paper on pan.

2. In small pan, add water or apple juice and dried apples and raisins. Heat for a few minutes to plump dried fruit. Turn off heat and let cool.

3. In a large mixing bowl, beat eggs and add oil, applesauce, and vanilla. Stir together.

4. Add flour, oatmeal, baking powder, cinnamon, and salt; mix well.

5. Add dried fruit mixture from saucepan. Mix to blend well. Add nuts (if using) and mix thoroughly.

6. Drop by teaspoonfuls onto cookie sheet and bake at 375° F for 9–12 minutes.

Makes: about 3 dozen cookies

Refrigerator Apple-Oatmeal Cookies

During the Middle Ages, the growing of apples, as well as other fruits, was taken over by monasteries. The monks experimented with different methods of making orchards more fruitful. Their early work with apple trees became the foundation of today's apple industry.

Ingredients

1 large cooking apple,
   peeled and chopped
½ cup dates, pitted
½ cup raisins
1 cup water
½ cup (1 stick) butter
2 eggs, beaten
1 teaspoon vanilla
1 cup flour
1 teaspoon baking powder
1 cup oatmeal (regular or quick)
½ teaspoon cinnamon
¼ teaspoon nutmeg
¾ cup chopped nuts

Tools & Equipment

2 quart saucepan
large mixing bowl
small bowl for
   beating eggs
measuring cups
   and spoons
mixing spoon
egg beater or mixer
cookie sheets

1. In 2 quart saucepan over medium high heat, bring water, apples, dates, and raisins to a boil. Reduce heat to low and simmer 3 minutes. Remove from heat. Add butter. Stir until melted. Pour into large bowl. Let cool.

2. Add beaten eggs and vanilla. Mix. Stir in flour, oatmeal, baking powder, cinnamon, nutmeg, and nuts. Stir until well blended.

3. Cover and refrigerate overnight.

4. Drop by heaping teaspoons 2 inches apart on greased cookie sheet.

5. Bake in 350° F oven for 10–12 minutes. Cool on racks.

Makes: about 3 dozen cookies

Mix-in-the Pan Fruit Bars

Over 500 years ago when Columbus set sail for America, apples were the most important cultivated fruit in Europe. When the settlers came to the New World, they brought with them apple slips in order to grow apples for cider. Their common drink in Europe was cider as their water supply was unfit to drink. Thus they thought the water in America would also be unacceptable.

Ingredients

1 cup dates, pitted
1 cup water
½ cup (1 stick) butter
2 eggs, beaten
1 teaspoon vanilla extract
1 cup flour
1 teaspoon baking powder
½ teaspoon cinnamon
¼ teaspoon nutmeg
¼ teaspoon salt
1 cup apples, sliced and
  cut in small pieces
½ cup chopped nuts

Tools & Equipment

7 x 11–inch baking pan
medium saucepan
kitchen scissors
cutting board
paring knife
measuring cups and
  spoons
mixing spoon
rubber scraper
small bowl for beating egg
egg beater

1. Use kitchen scissors to cut dates into small pieces. In medium saucepan over medium heat, bring water and dates to a boil. Reduce heat to medium low and simmer for 5 minutes. Add butter. Mix and set aside to cool.

2. Add eggs and vanilla to date mixture in pan.

3. Measure flour, baking powder, and salt. Add to mixture in pan. Stir in apples and nuts.

4. Spread in greased pan and bake in 350° F oven for 20–25 minutes.

Serves: 6–9 servings

Apple Chunky Bars

Apples have been attributed to a number of events in history. For example, did an apple really inspire Sir Isaac Newton to formulate the law of gravity? It is possible that as he sat in an orchard pondering the forces that attract objects to the earth, he saw an apple drop. This may have led him on a train of thought that evolved into his famous theory.

Ingredients

Filling

4 cups cooking apples, peeled
  and coarsely chopped
  (about 2 large or 3 medium
  apples)
¼ cup water
1 tablespoon honey
1 teaspoon cinnamon

Crust

2 cups oatmeal (regular or quick)
2 cups flour
1 teaspoon baking powder
1 teaspoon cinnamon
¾ cup butter (1½ sticks), softened
2 tablespoons cane sugar

Tools & Equipment

9 x 13–inch pan
cutting board
paring knife
medium saucepan
measuring cups
  and spoons
large mixing bowl
mixing spoon

1. Preheat oven to 350° F. Grease a 9 x 13–inch pan.

2. For *Filling*: combine apples, water, honey, and cinnamon in medium saucepan. Bring to a boil. Reduce heat and

simmer uncovered for 5 minutes or until apples are slightly softened. Remove from heat.

3. For *Crust*: in large mixing bowl, cream butter and cane sugar. Add oatmeal, flour, baking powder and cinnamon. Mix well to combine.

4. Set aside 2 cups of oat mixture for the topping.

5. Press remaining oat mixture into greased pan.

6. Bake for 12 minutes.

7. Spread cooked apple filling carefully over baked crust. Sprinkle reserved oat mixture over top.

8. Bake an additional 15–20 minutes or until top is nicely browned. Cool. Cut into bars.

Makes: 18–24 bars

Applesauce Bars

There were already wild crabapples growing in North America when the Pilgrims arrived, but they were small and sour. The apples the Pilgrims planted thrived in the cool climate of the East Coast. From this early start, America has never been without apples.

Ingredients

1 cup raisins
½ cup water
¼ cup (½ stick) butter
¾ cup applesauce, unsweetened
1 egg
1 cup all–purpose flour
1 teaspoon baking powder
1 teaspoon cinnamon
¼ teaspoon nutmeg
¼ teaspoon allspice
¼ teaspoon cloves
½ cup apple juice
¼ teaspoon vanilla

Tools & Equipment

9 x 9–inch pan
medium saucepan
mixing spoon
measuring cup and
 spoons
rubber scraper

1. Preheat oven to 350° F. Grease 9 x 9–inch pan.

2. In medium saucepan, heat raisins and water and boil for 3 minutes. Add butter and let melt. Cool.

3. Add applesauce to cooled mixture in pan. Stir in egg, flour, baking powder, spices, and blend well. Slowly add apple juice and vanilla. Mix well until combined.

4. Spread in pan. Bake for 25–30 minutes.

Makes 9–12 bars

Fast Apple Squares

Was there really such a man as Johnny Appleseed? He has become immortalized in song and story as a dedicated tree planter who traveled on foot through the hills and valleys of the eastern part of our country planting apple seeds.

Ingredients

¼ cup (½ stick) butter
¼ cup honey
1 egg, beaten
1 teaspoon vanilla
1 cup flour
1 teaspoon baking powder
½ teaspoon cinnamon
¼ teaspoon nutmeg
¼ teaspoon salt
1 medium apple, peeled and chopped
¼ cup nuts, chopped

Tools & Equipment

9 x 9–inch pan
medium saucepan
measuring cups
 and spoons
egg beater or mixer
mixing spoon
cutting board
paring knife

1. In medium saucepan, melt butter. Remove from heat and cool slightly. Add honey, beaten egg, and vanilla.

2. Stir in dry ingredients.

3. Blend in apple and chopped nuts.

4. Spread in greased 9 x 9–inch baking pan.

5. Bake in 350° F oven for 25–30 minutes or until toothpick inserted in center comes out clean. Cut into squares while warm.

Makes: 16 squares

Desserts

Cooked Applesauce

Try applesauce on toast, or with peanut butter in a sandwich (in place of the jelly). It's good on pancakes or waffles. Mix it into oatmeal or other hot cereal for breakfast. Freeze it and then whip in a blender for a spoon—eaten slushie. You might even like it spooned over ice cream or over vanilla pudding. It's good served over yogurt. There are lots of ways to enjoy applesauce. Of course, you can eat it plain, too.

Ingredients

4–6 medium cooking apples
  (Granny Smith, McIntosh, Jonathan,
  Winsap, Cortland, Rome Beauty)
½ cup water
½ teaspoon cinnamon

Tools & Equipment

cutting board
paring knife
medium saucepan
hand masher or
  blender or food
  processor

1. Wash and peel apples (or not). Cut into quarters and then cut out seeds and stems.

2. Put apples, water, and cinnamon into medium saucepan.

3. Cook over low heat until apples are soft, about 15 to 20 minutes. Watch carefully. **DO NOT LET APPLES SCORCH!**

4. After apples cool, break up with a hand masher or put in blender or food processor, depending how chunky or smooth you want the applesauce.

Crockpot® Applesauce

One pound of apples usually contains 4 small apples, or 3 medium, or 2 large apples, and yields approximately 3 cups of diced apples. Two medium apples yield approximately 1 cup of grated apple.

Ingredients
6 medium apples
½ cup water
1–2 teaspoons cinnamon
1 tablespoon honey

Tools & Equipment
Crockpot®
mixing spoon
cutting board
paring knife

1. Peel and core apples. Cut apples into chunky pieces and place in Crockpot®.
2. Add water, cinnamon, and honey to apples and stir together until apples are evenly coated.
3. Cover Crockpot® and cook on low for 4 hours or until soft.
4. Mash with a hand masher until the desired degree of chunky–ness. Use a mixer for creamier applesauce.
5. Store in the refrigerator for 4–5 days or in the freezer for several months.

"I tell you, all politics is applesauce." Will Rogers

Baked Apple Halves

Apples contain an impressive list of phtyto–nutrients, and anti–oxidants. Studies suggest this is necessary for normal growth, development and overall well–being. Apples are low in calories, having only about 80 calories per medium apple, and contain no saturated fats or cholesterol. They are high in vitamin A and C and also contain a small amount of minerals like potassium, phosphorus, and calcium. What a bargain in weight control and nutrition!

Ingredients

2 cooking apples
¼ teaspoon cinnamon
¼ cup orange juice
½ cup water
2 tablespoons raisins (optional)

Tools & Equipment

8 x 8–inch baking pan or
 4 custard cups
cutting board
paring knife

1. Preheat oven to 350° F. Have ready an 8 x 8–inch baking pan or 4 custard cups.

2. Cut apples in half lengthwise (core to stem) and remove core but do not peel.

3. Lay the apples skin side down (cavity up) on baking pan or in custard cups. Sprinkle with cinnamon. Spoon raisins into center of each. Pour orange juice over apples and water around apples.

4. Bake for 20–30 minutes or until apples are tender but still hold their shape.

Makes 2–4 servings

Apple Brown Betty

The definition of a Brown Betty is a fruit dish (apples, berries, peaches), baked between layers of buttered crumbs. The Betty was a popular baked pudding during colonial times in America. Here is an updated version.

Ingredients

3 or 4 apples
¼ cup frozen apple juice
concentrate, thawed
½ teaspoon cinnamon
1 cup flour
¼ cup cane sugar
1 teaspoon baking powder
¼ teaspoon salt
6 tablespoons (¾ stick)
  butter

Tools & Equipment

9 x 9–inch pan
  cutting board,
paring knife
small bowl
medium bowl
measuring cups
  and spoons
2 knives or pastry
  blender

1. Lightly grease 9 x 9–inch pan

2. Peel and slice apples. In medium bowl toss apples with apple juice and cinnamon. Arrange in pan.

3. In small mixing bowl, mix together flour and cane sugar. Cut in butter with 2 knives or pastry blender. Mixture will be crumbly. Sprinkle over apples in pan.

4. Bake in 350° F oven for 35–40 minutes or until lightly browned.

Makes: 9 servings

Apple Pandowdy

Apple Pandowdy is another old–time name for an apple dish. It is generally considered to be a deep dish dessert made with apples (or other fruit for a different Pandowdy–taste) sweetened with brown sugar or molasses. The topping is a crumbly type of biscuit. If the apples are juicy enough, the topping is pushed down into the fruit to allow the juices to come through. The name Pandowdy is thought to refer to desserts that are rather plain or dowdy–looking in appearance.

Ingredients

¼ cup cane sugar
2 tablespoons flour
½ teaspoon cinnamon
¼ teaspoon salt
1 cup water
2 tablespoons butter
1 teaspoon vanilla
2 large (or 3 small) apples,
   peeled and sliced

Tools & Equipment

9–inch square pan
cutting board
paring knife
medium saucepan
small mixing bowl & fork
measuring cups & spoons
egg beater

Batter

1 beaten egg
⅓ cup milk
1 cup flour
2 teaspoons baking powder
¼ teaspoon salt
3 tablespoons melted butter

1. In medium saucepan, mix together cane sugar, flour, cinnamon, and salt. Stir in water. Cook on medium heat until mixture boils and is slightly thickened. Stir often so mixture gets smooth and doesn't burn on the bottom. Remove from burner and stir in butter and vanilla.

2. Peel and slice apples into a buttered 9–inch square pan.

3. Pour sauce over apples. Meanwhile, prepare batter by beating egg in small bowl, adding milk and stir with fork to blend.

4. Into egg–milk mixture, add flour, cane sugar, baking powder, and salt. Mix slightly. Add melted butter.

5. Stir with a fork to make a drop batter. **Do NOT overmix**.

6. Bake in 375° F oven for 30–35 minutes.

7. Can be served right side up or upside down with the apples on top.

Apple Crisp

Crisps are desserts that have a fruit mixture on the bottom and a crumb mixture on top. The crumbs can be made with flour, bread crumbs, cracker crumbs or breakfast cereal. Here you have one with flour and oatmeal. A Crumble is a British version of the American Crisp.

Ingredients

Filling

5–6 apples, peeled and
   sliced
½ cup frozen apple
   juice concentrate, thawed
½ teaspoon cinnamon
⅛ teaspoon salt

Tools & Equipment

9 x 13–inch pan
cutting board
paring knife
medium bowl
pastry blender or
   two knives

Topping

1 cup flour
1 cup oatmeal, quick or regular
¼ to ½ cup cane sugar
1 teaspoon baking powder
½ cup butter, (1 stick) cut in small
   pieces

1. Lightly grease a 9 x 13–inch pan.
2. Add peeled and sliced apples to mixing bowl. Add juice, cinnamon, and salt to apples; toss gently to coat. Spread apples in baking dish.

3. In bowl, combine flour, oatmeal, cane sugar, and baking powder. Cut in butter with pastry blender or two knives until clumps form. Sprinkle over apple mixture.

4. Bake in 375° F oven for 35 minutes or until lightly brown and apples are tender. Serve warm or cold.

Makes 12 servings

Snacks

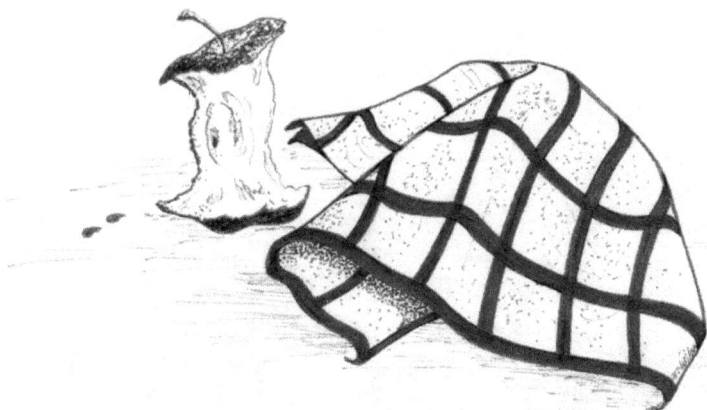

Chewy Gummies

Kids love to be creative with these chewy gummies.

Ingredients
3 cups apple juice
5 packets unflavored gelatin
  powder

Tools & Equipment
8 x 8–inch pan
small saucepan
cookie cutters

1. Combine 1 cup juice with the 5 packets of gelatin. In small saucepan, bring 1 cup juice to a boil. (*Adult will need to do this*). Stir in the gelatin mix. Add remaining apple juice.

2. Pour into an 8 x 8–inch pan and refrigerate until set. Kids get to use cookie cutters to cut out designs.

Fruit and Cheese Spikes

Encourage restaurants to add more fresh fruit to their menu. If customers keep requesting, restaurants will increase their selections. Consumers continue to be health conscience and look to fruit as an important aid to good nutrition.

Ingredients
1–2 eating–in–hand apples
pineapple chunks
fresh or canned peaches
cheese, your favorite

Tools & Equipment
cutting board
paring knife
small bowl
toothpicks or
    kabob sticks

1. Wash, core, and slice apples.
2. Let apples soak in pineapple or orange juice for a few minutes. Drain.
3. Cut cheese into small cubes or chunks.
4. On toothpick or kabob stick, alternate fruit with cheese chunks.

Apple Juice Popsicles®

Here are two recipes to have ready for the hot days of summer.

Ingredients

1 (48 ounce) jar or can of apple or cran–apple juice
12 (4 ounce) plastic glasses
12 teaspoons, to be used as popsicle® "handles"

Tools & Equipment

12 (4 ounce) plastic glasses
12 teaspoons

1. Pour apple juice into glasses.

2. Put teaspoon into each glass.

3. Set juice–filled glasses in level space in freezer.

4. Freeze for 4–5 hours or overnight.

5. When ready to eat, hold glass under hot water for a few seconds until popsicle® loosens.

Yield: 12 popsicles®

Apple Freezies

Ingredients

1 cup applesauce,
  unsweetened
1 cup apple juice or cider
1 cup water

Small paper cups or molds
Popsicle®–like sticks

Tools & Equipment

blender

Blend all in a blender until smooth. Pour into molds, add sticks, and freeze.

How to Dry Apples

Drying apples is a fun fall activity. They make healthy and low—fat, no—sugar treats.

There are a number of ways to dry apples: in a food dehydrator, an oven, and out in the sun. Here are directions for oven drying.

1. Wash apples but you do not need to peel them.

2. Core them and cut into thin slices. Keep the slices even.

3. Dip apples in a solution of water and a little lemon juice to keep them from turning brown. Or you can use a little orange juice or pineapple juice in water.

4. Turn oven to lowest temperature, about 170° F if possible, or super low. Spread well drained apples in a single layer on cooling racks set over large cookie sheets. Or you can use a screen from a retired food dehydrator or a new, clean window screen. Keep the door slightly open to allow moist air to escape. Having a fan by the door also helps to circulate the air. You'll have to turn them periodically and watch them closely if the heat has been turned higher.

5. It will take about 8–10 hours to dry apples in the oven. The higher the heat, the faster they will dry, but be careful not to burn them. They should feel leathery and almost crisp. It depends, too, on how you like

them. This does mean you will need to attend to them, know how they are doing, and turn off the oven when you sleep or leave the house.

Some like to dry apples outside in the sun. Here is an idea for you:

Use a bed sheet spread out on the trampoline. There should be a good circulation of air and direct sunlight. Use a wire screen to place over them to keep the flies and other flying critters off.

Apple Leather Roll-Ups

When I was teaching foods and nutrition my students enjoyed making and eating this version of the popular fruit roll–up. After they made the applesauce they prepared it for the roll–ups. The next day they sampled and had little snack bags to take home, if any were left!.

1. Make applesauce as on page 106.
2. Cover a 14 x 16–inch cookie sheet with heavy plastic food–grade wrap or parchment paper.
3. Add about a tablespoon honey to applesauce to keep it pliable when dried.
4. Spread evenly on the cookie sheet so that fruit is no more than ¼ inch thick.
5. Dry mixture in a 150° F oven for 6–8 hours. Prop door of oven open slightly to allow the moisture to escape.
6. After 6–8 hours, the mixture should be rubbery and slightly sticky.
7. While warm, peel the slab from the pan, roll up, and cut into small rolls or bars and store in refrigerator.
8. Can be placed in freezer bags and stored in freezer.
9. For variety, add well chopped nuts to the applesauce before drying.

Apple Chips

This is an interesting version of chips. Try it. I think you'll like it!

Ingredients
2 large apples, such as Delicious
½ teaspoon cinnamon
oil spray

1. Slice apples crosswise into very thin slices (⅛ inch).
   Place apples in a single layer on parchment–lined
   cookie sheets. Sprinkle cinnamon over and spray with
   oil.
2. Bake in 200° F oven until apples are dry and crisp. This
   will take about 4 hours or longer if they are cut a little
   thicker.
3. Let chips cool before transferring to a sealed container
   for up to 3 days.

Makes: about 2 cups of apple chips.

Other Books by Lee Jackson

From the Apple Orchard – Recipes for Apple Lovers

Midwest Independent Publishers Association (MIPA) First Place Award winner. This classic apple cookbook answers the question: *"What will I do with all these apples?"* Whether you have a bushel, a peck, or only a pound, you will find hundreds of ways to use apples. It's the perfect way to enjoy apple season all year around. Handy guide for choosing apples is included. To learn more go to:

http://www.imagesunlimitedpublishing.com

Apples, Apples Everywhere – Favorite Recipes From America's Orchard

Mid–America Publishers Association Award winner.
Some of the country's largest orchards, as well as small family businesses showcase their favorite apple recipes. You will see where they are located and read a short history of each orchard. It's like taking a tour through America's orchards and picking your favorite apples and recipes along the way. To learn more go to:

http://www.imagesunlimitedpublishing.com

Careers in Focus – Family and Consumer Sciences

Missouri Writers Guild Major Work Award winner. This textbook offers guidelines for succeeding in the world of work. It surveys key careers in family and consumer sciences and shows you how to develop job skills to achieve success in any field. The key activities guide you in finding a satisfying career by helping you identify your personality traits, interests, aptitudes and skills. Skills and work attitudes necessary for job success are emphasized. Positive work habits and attitudes influence success in any field.

Selected careers are identified in business and marketing, education and communication, human services, science and technology, the arts, and entrepreneurship. For more information go to:

http://www.g-w.com/careers-in-focus-2008

The Littlest Christmas Kitten

First Place MIPA Award Winner in Children's Picture Books. In this retelling of the birth of Christ a mother cat searches frantically for her little lost kitten. Before the night is over there is the crying of a baby and angels singing His praises. Animal witnesses to the nativity are in awe as they pay homage to this special baby. The night's events leave a lasting effect on all the animals, especially the cats.

Illustrator Kelly Dupre uses colorful, bold, and playful wood cut original illustrations to reflect the importance of that Holy Night. Visit Lee Jackson's blog at:

http://cookingandkids.com/blog

For more information go to:

http://www.imagesunlimitedpublishing.com

Books are available at libraries, selected book-stores, Amazon, or directly from the publisher at Images Unlimited Publishing, P.O. Box 305, Maryville, MO 64468 660-582-4605 info@imagesunlimitedpub.com

Recipe Index

Images Unlimited Order Form

Yes, I want to order **books** for kids, families and teachers. Send me:

Qty	Title	Price	Total
_____	**Healthy to the Core! All Natural Low Sugar/ No Sugar Apple Recipes For Kids** kids love apples – now recipes with less sugar, healthier	$ 14.95	_____
_____	**From the Apple Orchard — Recipes for Apple Lovers**, revised and expanded classic apple cookbook	14.95	_____
_____	**Apples, Apples Everywhere — Favorite Recipes From America's Orchards**, apple growers best recipes	14.95	_____
_____	**Apples,** wonderful little book with colored apple pictures, apple history, and apple lore	17.95	_____
_____	**Our Apple Tree,** children ages 3–12 learn about the life of the apple tree and the animals that visit	7.99	_____
_____	**Cooking Around the Calendar With Kids — Holiday and Seasonal Food and Fun,** cooking & fun with children all year	12.95	_____
_____	**Cooking Around the Country With Kids USA Regional Recipes and Fun Activities,** take a food and fun tour through the USA	19.95	_____
_____	**Listening to the Mukies and Their Character Building Adventures,** read–aloud stories about relationships	12.95	_____
_____	**The Littlest Christmas Kitten,** children's full color storybook about the night Jesus was born and the kittens reaction	16.00	_____

Shipping:

Up to $50…$6.50
$51 to $100…9.00
$2 per book thereafter

Subtotal _____
Shipping _____
Missouri residents add 7.975% tax _____
TOTAL _____

Name _____

Street _____

City _____ State _____ Zip _____

Charge to _____ Visa _____ M/C Acct# _____

Exp. Date: _____ Name on card _____

Or make check or money order payable to:
Images Unlimited, P.O. Box 305, Maryville, MO 64468   800-366-1695
Visit us on the web at http://www.ImagesUnlimitedPublishing.com and
http://www.CookingandKids.com/blog

www.ingramcontent.com/pod-product-compliance
Lightning Source LLC
LaVergne TN
LVHW021518080426
835509LV00018B/2552